Summary

T0373052

This guide is for local authorities, owners and others involved in the conservation of Georgian and Victorian / early 20th century terraced housing. It gives a historic overview of terraced housing and identifies important features of different types of terrace.

It will help local authorities and others implementing historic environment legislation and policy.

It will also help those planning to make changes to terraced housing to understand their buildings and what is special about them. It identifies issues to consider for those wishing to make alterations and it provides helpful information for making planning applications.

This document has been prepared by Nigel Barker-Mills, Duncan McCallum, Victoria Thomson, Robyn Pender, Michael Dunn and Kate Guest. This edition published by Historic England July 2020. All images © Historic England unless otherwise stated.

Please refer to this document as:
Historic England 2020 Conserving Georgian and Victorian terraced housing. Swindon. Historic England.

https://historicengland.org.uk/images-books/publications/conserving-georgian-victorian-terraced-housing

Front cover:
Lansdown Hill, Bath.

Contents

Introduction

1

This guide aims to support those involved in the conservation of Georgian and Victorian / early 20th century terraced housing (1715 – c1919). We anticipate that it will be of most use to owners of historic terraces and local authorities dealing with requests for listed building consent.

It will help with implementing historic environment legislation, policy in the National Planning Policy Framework (NPPF) and related guidance given in the Planning Practice Guidance (NPPG). In addition to these, this guide is designed to be read in conjunction with the relevant Good Practice Advice and Historic England Advice Notes.

The guide emphasises that evidence required to inform decisions affecting terraced housing should be proportionate to the importance of the asset.

Georgian and Victorian / early 20th century terraced housing encompasses a wide variety of types and there will be some variation in importance. A range of factors determine the significance of any historic building and it is necessary to understand the importance of an individual asset before considering changes. This will help decision makers to determine how easily a particular building will absorb change. It is therefore not the intention of this guide to provide hard and fast rules about acceptable levels of change, but rather to set out the issues and the areas of the terraced house which decision makers need to consider when deciding whether change is acceptable.

Figure 1:
Different types of Georgian and Victorian terraces are found across the country.

The focus of this document is on listed terraces which are subject to statutory protection and included on the National Heritage List for England. It highlights particular issues to consider when sustaining the heritage significance of this distinct building type. The basic principles can also apply to other historic terraces, for example those in conservation areas, of which there are numerous examples across the country.

Terraced housing is found across England, having first emerged as a building type in the late 17th century. An essential characteristic of the terrace is the desire for consistency, either for architectural or commercial reasons. This results in a limited number of closely related plan forms. This guide defines terraced housing as:

> *"development which comprises three or more uniformly designed houses sharing common materials, boundary treatments and plan forms. The terraced house is essentially an urban building type, particularly characteristic of cites and major towns, although examples can be found in smaller market towns and villages."*

This guide supersedes the English Heritage publication 'London Terraced Housing 1660 -1860'.

2 Historic overview

The development of towns in England created many terraced houses, ranging from grand aristocratic compositions intended to mimic country houses through to modest workers' housing. The terraced house was a particularly important urban form, and a substantial portion of listed domestic buildings falls into this category. The Georgian terrace has long been regarded as England's greatest contribution to the urban form, defining and shaping the historic character of places like London, Bath, Manchester, Leeds, Newcastle and Brighton, where whole districts of terraces still exist.

2.1 Georgian period

Regular terraces first appeared in the later 17th century. These early buildings were designed for an educated elite, and were based on continental classical models, most probably inspired by Inigo Jones' work at Covent Garden. Interest in the terrace form intensified after the Restoration of the Monarchy, and the late 17th century saw the rise of large-scale, speculative builders in London (such as Nicholas Barbon, who played a role in the reconstruction of London following the Great Fire in 1666). This encouraged standardisation in plan and appearance.

Early Building Acts from 1667 onwards divided the London terrace into four classes, defined by the number of storeys, ceiling heights, wall thicknesses, and road widths. The influence of these Acts – which at the time only applied to the City of London – spread across the capital and out to other parts of the country.

Figure 2:
A very early 1690s terrace in Bideford, Devon.

Figure 3:
The Royal Crescent in Bath is one of the most famous terraces in the country.

Technological advances made this increased level of development possible. The drop in the price of glass meant that windows could be made large enough to illuminate the floor space and stairs from only two walls. This was coupled with the invention of the sash window, which allowed for effective ventilation of the floor plate.

By the early 18th century fashionable terraces, designed to impress, were being constructed in London and Bath with other early examples surviving in cities such as Bristol (Queen's Square, dated1699-1727). These were often built during periods of increased economic prosperity. By the middle of the century, terraces were evolving into grander compositions, including circuses and crescents. This architecture – so integral to the character of Bath, and associated with its status as a fashionable spa – was imitated in other resorts, including Buxton, Brighton, Hastings, Leamington and Cheltenham.

In London, more rigorous enforcement of the Building Acts after 1774 led to simplification, and an increased consistency in the external appearance of the many more modest terraces being constructed by speculative builders. These were often grey or stock brick, with decoration confined to entrances and boundary treatments such as railings. In the interiors of the houses, panelling, fireplaces and staircases conformed to a standard vocabulary and disposition.

At the same time, the grand terrace composition intended for wealthy households also flourished. The terraces of Nash and Cubitt were based on the precedent set by Robert Adam at the Adelphi in London and had grand aspirations towards changing the character of London as part of major townscape remodelling. Examples are found in other cities too, including the work of Robert Grainger in Newcastle and John Foster in Liverpool. By the late Georgian and early Victorian period many towns across the country, including York, Exeter, Hull, Liverpool and Leeds, had handsome streets for the wealthier urban class lined with the ordered facades of terraced development.

2.2 Victorian period

During the Victorian period populations in London, Liverpool and other northern cities rapidly expanded as part of industrialisation and developing commerce. Large numbers of terraces were built speculatively to accommodate householders at the lower end of the socio-economic scale, who required accommodation close to their places of work. Examples of this type of terrace can be found in the dockland areas of east London and around the factories of Yorkshire and Lancashire. At the same time, the terrace form was also used for model communities sponsored by enlightened mill owners and employers like Titus Salt (who constructed Saltaire for his workforce).

The grand architectural terrace began to decline after the middle of the 19th century, as the rich turned more towards individual houses. Terraces then became more closely associated with the aspiring middle classes. Mid-Victorian terraces increasingly used stucco and Italianate styles, examples of which can be found not only in suburban areas like the 1850s terraces in Sunderland or the 1860s housing in Leeds, but also in emerging coastal resorts such as Teignmouth in Devon and Fleetwood in Lancashire.

Figure 4:
Smaller, standardised terraces were associated with factory and mill workers.

By the later Victorian period, the upper middle classes too were generally seeking detached houses or villas. The terrace then became associated with the lower middle classes, but retained a form and quality that distinguished them from the cheap, standardised 'byelaw' row houses built for workers close to the factories and mills. 'Byelaw' housing usually refers to housing built to comply with the Public Health Act 1875, which imposed certain standards on quality. By the end of the 19th century terraces had become very accurate illustrations of the social and economic standing of the areas in which they were found, which adds to their historic interest.

Following the end of the First World War and the advent of new housing legislation in 1919, Victorian terraces became associated with overcrowding and slums. Terraces gave way to the rise of semi-detached houses.

Although consistency and standardisation are key characteristics of terrace development through the centuries, regional variations were developed that led to distinct urban types. The urban mews, for example (which provided a solution to stabling in a dense urban setting) is predominantly found in London, although there are examples in Brighton and Bath. The development of 'back to back' terraces, with houses sharing a rear party wall, is a distinctive feature of several northern towns and cities, especially Leeds and West Yorkshire. In the north-east of the country, 'Tyneside Flats' and the 'Sunderland Cottage', which comprised rows of bungalows, are also distinctive; the London version is 'Cottage flats'. These forms are all testament to the variety, efficiency and inherent adaptability of the terrace, which has enabled it to survive successfully to the present day.

3 An approach to change

A key challenge when planning change to terrace development is reaching a balance between meeting the needs of owners whilst sustaining the consistency of external architecture, internal plan and internal detail that distinguishes this building type. The standardisation of plan and use of modest materials in many terraces can lead to an under-appreciation of the value and interest of the individual house as contributing to a greater whole. A good starting point is to establish as far as is reasonable the intentions of the original developer of the terrace, placing it within its historical and social context. This will then assist understanding of the importance of the plan form, the materials used, boundary treatment and the wider role of the house as part of the terrace in the street and immediate context.

Understanding the distinctive nature of the architectural and historic significance of terraced houses is important. It can help to understand how adaptable they may be and therefore improve their viability and long-term prospects. Successful proposals deliver the mutually supportive objectives of economic, social and environmental gains together wherever possible. Conservation involves managing change in such a way that the significance of heritage assets is sustained or even enhanced. With careful consideration based upon a good understanding, changes can avoid or minimise harm. Where there will be harm, this requires clear and convincing justification.

The emergence of terraced housing is largely based upon its efficiency in meeting the distinctively English custom for individual housing in an urban context. Its survival is based upon its adaptability in meeting later fashions and changing use.

In many cases there are also opportunities to restore lost elements eroded through past changes and enhance the significance of not just the individual house, but the terrace as a whole.

Where like-for-like repairs are being considered, Historic England recommends that the materials used match the original materials as closely as possible. Materials which match in both appearance and physical properties will react and weather the same way over time.

Where there is a cluster of listed buildings in an area, local authorities may wish to consider Local Listed Building Consent Orders (LLBCOs) or Heritage Partnership Agreements (HPAs). LLBCOs allow local authorities to grant listed building consent for specific works to groups of listed buildings in all or part of their area. This means that owners will not need to make individual applications but can proceed with works, subject to any conditions that may be attached to the order. HPAs allow local authorities to grant listed building consent for specific works agreed with the owner/s of a building for an extended period of time. For more information, see the Historic England Advice Note.

When considering change to terraced housing, the following aspects of their architectural and historic interest require particular consideration.

3.1 Plan form

The basic plan form of the regular terraced house of the Georgian period (1715-1840) is usually two rooms deep but often with cellar or basement below. The ground and first floors of Georgian terraced houses were often the most significant. These housed service or ancillary rooms in the upper floors of larger houses or in a rear extension and below for smaller houses. There are a limited number of related plan forms with a consistent hierarchy between front and back rooms. The width of the plan was unusually consistent, particularly in London, although depth could be more variable.

The standard terrace house plan of the Victorian period (1840-c1900) for the middle class and workers' housing is two floors of two rooms each, with the entrance hall and stairs to one side. Variants usually comprise further floors on top, basements below and extensions to the rear. A major exception to this common plan is the central entrance plan with the stair rising immediately behind the front door lobby and two main windows on each floor. Terrace plans with no hall and direct entrance to the front room, often called the 'parlour', are generally indicative of workers' housing.

The example terraced house below shows some of the areas and features, found in many terrace types, to consider when planning changes to a property. It shows areas where it may be possible to retain, repair or reinstate original features and some areas where there may be opportunity for change. The relevant part of the guidance note then provides more detail about types of issue to consider when planning change.

Existing roof form and structure retained and repaired with appropriate materials

Redundant tanks or boilers removed to increase capacity in the roof

Opportunities to retain or reinstate original plan form, floor structures, walls, staircases, and internal partitions

Openings in partitions may be formed in partition walls and modern partitions removed

Changes affecting party walls will require careful planning

Potential opportunities for carefully considered work to improve environmental performance while retaining historic fabric

New brickwork matching or toned down to match original

Existing window and door joinery retained or details reinstated

Vaults, front basements, stone paving, pavement lights, coal hole covers and domestic features retained or repaired

Figure 5:
Example cut away terraced house: typical features and issues to consider when planning changes

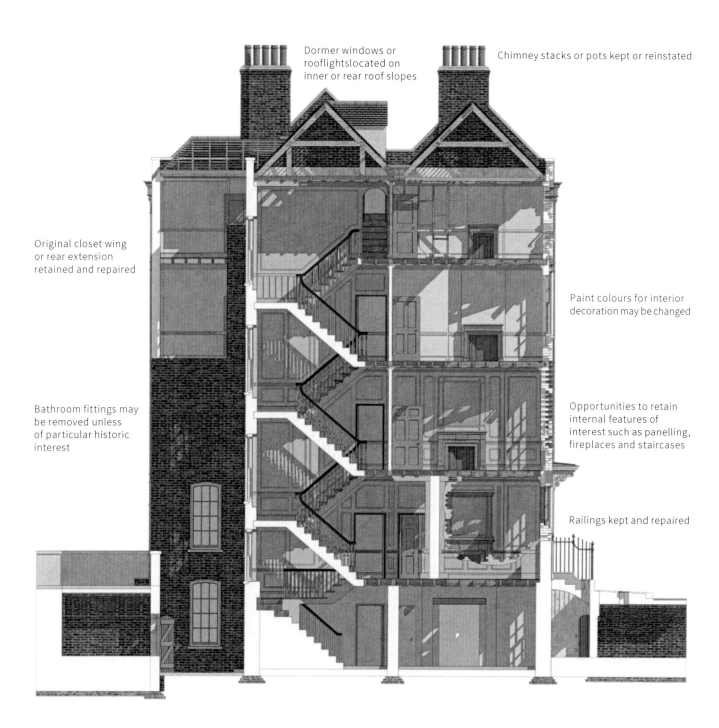

Dormer windows or rooflightslocated on inner or rear roof slopes

Chimney stacks or pots kept or reinstated

Original closet wing or rear extension retained and repaired

Paint colours for interior decoration may be changed

Bathroom fittings may be removed unless of particular historic interest

Opportunities to retain internal features of interest such as panelling, fireplaces and staircases

Railings kept and repaired

Changes can increase capacity of vaults and basements while retaining historic fabric

3.1.1 Stairs

The position of the staircase within a plan could vary. Early terrace plans often had the stair in the centre of the house between the front and back room accessed by a passage between. In London by 1700 this was generally superseded by the side hall and stair which remained consistent through to the Victorian period. For smaller terrace plans stairs could often be in the rear room on the side with usually one turn at the top (a 'dog-leg'). For larger terraces, including those with basements, the stairs are usually double flight with landings and are lit by large windows in the rear elevation.

In London, the leasehold system of speculative terrace housing could result in the upgrading of houses to reflect changing fashion at the end of a lease, rather than complete redevelopment. It is therefore common to find earlier plans behind later elevations and staircases are often a useful indicator of date. Smaller separate stairs to attics and service rooms were often left in place even if the rest of the house underwent a thorough internal re-ordering: where they survive they make an important contribution to significance.

3.1.2 Interior features

Terraced house interiors often have a standard vocabulary of typical patterns of panelling, cornices, fireplaces and skirtings. These often reflect the hierarchy of rooms, being simpler in what were seen as less important areas. Earlier examples of interior features would often be hand crafted, but by the later 18th century and into the 19th century elements such as stair balusters would be 'machined'.

3.1.3 Basements and cellars

Many urban houses were built with rooms below the level of the street with only a simple window and sometimes access from the front. The relationship between this lowest level of the building and the street was not always straightforward and some terraces have half-basements or cellars. The full basement, which broadly follows the dimensions of the rooms above, is characteristic of Georgian urban terraces, particularly in London. It usually originally contained the kitchen at the back, servants' hall at the front or, for smaller houses, the breakfast room. There is often access from the basement to the rear yard and, in London, access from the street. In order to provide front access and to allow for a proper window the 'area' was created. In London and some other urban centres larger houses extend the 'area' forward under the footpath or street for storage, for example of coal. The 'area' is an important transition zone between the street and the house providing functional and physical separation and increasing the comfort of the occupants.

Figure 6:
Black railings maintain the uniformity of basement flat entrances.

Basement vaults are an important feature of the planning of some types of Georgian and Victorian terraced house. They are a characteristic feature of the construction of terraced housing in Bath and surrounding districts. They were often originally built to support the highway above and provided the house with a service area and coal storage.

3.1.4 Kitchens and service rooms

The aim of most terraced house plans was to place service or rooms for ancillary functions out of sight and distinct from the main living area of the house. In the larger Georgian terrace, supported by a significant complement of household staff, the accommodation for servants would often be in the basement along with the kitchen, pantry and scullery.

In houses without basements and those of smaller size, service rooms such as sculleries and kitchens were placed to the rear, often in an extension, with further accommodation for servants in the upper floors. The rear of a Georgian terrace is generally easier to alter without compromising architectural integrity. Extensions are therefore often later than the main range, or have been substantially altered over the years to accommodate improvements in sanitation and comfort.

For terraces in the Victorian period, particularly those for the middle class and workers' housing, the rear 'extension' was often provided in a consistent manner (for example coupled under one roof) and the distinction between a consistent façade and an informal, incremental rear elevation is not so distinct.

Figure 7:
Rear view of a terrace showing different alterations and extensions.

If there are plans to change the plan form, issues to consider include, but are not exclusive to, the following:

1. Will the proposal involve the erosion of the original plan?

2. Will the proposal involve the loss of the last surviving element of the plan?

3. Are there opportunities to re-instate elements of the former plan?

4. Does the proposal involve loss of the stairs or part of the stair?

5. How will the proposal change the relationship between the house and the street?

6. Is the original hierarchy of rooms still present?

7. Are changes to the original hierarchy themselves important?

8. How does the proposal affect the ability to appreciate earlier change?

9. How will the proposal affect the relationship between the main rooms and service rooms of the house?

10. How will the proposal affect surviving interior fittings including fireplaces, cornices, skirting boards, panelling and shutters?

11. Are there opportunities to accurately re-instate missing interior features?

3.2 Elevations

The speculative system that underlies the creation of the terrace was based on ensuring consistency in the overall composition of the front elevation. In its earliest form this was based on the order and composition of the classical tradition. Architectural styles and fashion changed in the Victorian period but the underlying desire for consistency within a terrace development remained.

For the terraces of the Regency period (c1810-30) and later, when the use of stucco and render became particularly fashionable, consistency of finish was even more important and the use of colour was often controlled. Original finishes imitating stone or more expensive materials were often used but the majority have now been covered over or lost. Features such as balconies enlivening the façade were also popular, especially in seaside and spa towns. In other urban centres architectural detail (including window surrounds and drips, cornices and string courses) was consistent, often providing the only decoration in otherwise sober brick facades, alongside their function in providing protection from the weather.

Figure 8:
The front of a terrace usually showcases the consistency of the development.

3.2.1 Roofs

Of particular importance in the elevation was the treatment of the roof, which for those terraces employing the classical tradition was often hidden behind a parapet. Late Georgian terraces across the country usually reflected the hierarchy of the interior plan in their window proportions. But the roof, even when visible, was often kept to a low, usually uninterrupted pitch. This ensured the visual dominance of features such a pediments or attics which were deliberately designed as architectural emphases to be seen from a distance. In more modest terraces dormer windows allowed the use of the roof space for ancillary accommodation but were typically small in size and discreetly placed.

In the mid and late Victorian periods different, more decorative architectural styles (including forms of Gothic Revival and Queen Anne Revival) place greater importance on the use of gables, bays and roofs, delighting in the opportunities for ornament and detail. These were also usually treated consistently within an individual terrace. Regional variations in the use of materials can also be found in the Victorian period. These include combining different stones or different, often contrasting coloured bricks (polychrome brickwork) with stone dressings, adding to the architectural interest.

Issues to be considered regarding elevations:

1. Will the proposal erode the consistency of the elevation treatment, such as the treatment of windows or colour?

2. Is the external colour treatment controlled by lease or covenant?

3. Will the proposal accurately restore lost features enhancing architectural consistency?

4. Will the proposal involve increasing the prominence of the roof on the front elevation?

5. Will the proposal respect and/or complement existing materials?

3.3 Extensions

The front elevations of many Georgian terraces were the result of a combination of factors including Building Acts, leasehold requirements and architectural economy. The desire for regularity applied mainly to front elevations but greater change was permitted to the rear. The rear rooms were usually lower status and often contained service rooms such as pantries, sculleries and kitchens. Early service or 'closet' wings are now unusual and important where they survive.

The back extensions are often the most varied and complicated part of terraced houses and have been subject to the most change. Later Georgian and Regency terraced houses have often had their rear yards infilled with a variety of additions and in medium sized Georgian houses there was often a basement level rear extension with a single storey 'back room' above at ground floor. Outside of London or where land was at less of a premium many terraces could have longer extensions of varying heights.

After the middle of the 19th century the back extension became more regular, often two-storeyed, and the use of basements declined, with the kitchen and sculleries now being placed on the ground floor at the rear. The rear extension also became more consistent in plan in the interests of economy. In more modest examples the 'coupled' single-roofed extension emerged, placed across the rear of two adjacent houses that shared the same yard.

Although the rear of terraces is usually the area that has been most altered it is important that any proposals for further extensions or alterations respect existing important fabric and surviving internal features to ensure an appropriate relationship is maintained between the main house, rear extensions and the original extent of the yard or garden.

Issues to be considered when extending terrace houses:

1. Are existing extensions historically significant?

2. Is there an existing rhythm to the extensions?

3. Does the proposal enclose or infill the rear yard?

4. Does the service character of the extension survive ie small simple, unadorned rooms?

5. How does proposal affect the traditional service character of the extension?

6. What is the impact upon the balance between main house and rear extension?

7. What is the impact upon surviving interior features?

3.4 The terrace and the street

As an urban building type, the relationship between the terrace and the street is an important element of its special interest. The architectural consistency of the terrace extended to the treatment of boundaries when private space began to be created, which was usually outside city centres. Where the terrace faces directly onto a front garden or area this space provides an important transition between public and private zones and maintaining a distinct defined boundary was important. Original boundary treatments (which could include dwarf walls with metal railings, stone balustrades or hedges) were usually treated as part of the architectural composition and would also become simpler further down the 'class' of terrace.

Figure 9:
The boundary treatment for this terrace is a wall with railings.

Figure 10:
A row of terraces facing onto a garden area.

A notable variation to the suburban street of terraces is the northern street block comprising 'back-to-back' houses, with no rear gardens; sometimes enclosing a central yard or court used for toilets or drying. There are some alternative layouts for terraces off 'courts', ie not directly accessed from the public street.

The grandest late Georgian and Regency terraces faced onto a square or garden, which often was a private amenity only accessible by keyholders. A variant was the creation of a semi-private lawn or greenery placed between the driveway to the terrace and the public road, as found for example in Leamington Spa and Cheltenham. These spaces add to the architectural and historic interest of the terrace and are key elements of their setting.

In the 19th century some terraces could be placed within their own park, accessed by private roads, but by the end of the century all medium sized houses and the majority of smaller houses were built with a front garden with a consistent boundary treatment as well as the rear yard or garden.

3.4.1 Mews

The Georgian and Regency terraced houses intended for the wealthiest occupiers had their own stables and accommodation for coachmen at the end of the rear yard to the house, with access to a small back street or mews. The physical separation between the main house and these service buildings was important and the entrance to the mews was often embellished with an ornamental or imposing gateway. Outside of London mews are quite rare, but examples can be found such as those in Brighton. Separate rear access to later medium sized and smaller terraced housing became rarer from the middle of the 19th century in the south of England, although in the industrial terraces of the north the rear access or back lane became an important part of the urban grain.

Issues to consider when considering changes which affect the relationship between the terrace and the street:

1. What is the impact of proposals on boundary walls/fences?
2. Are any of those boundaries party walls?
3. Will the proposal reinstate missing boundary features?
4. Will the proposal substantially infill the garden space?
5. Will the proposal link formerly separate mews?

Figure 11:
View of a London mews.

3.5 Maintenance and environmental performance

Good conservation of heritage assets is founded on appropriate routine management and maintenance. Such an approach will minimise the need for larger repairs or other interventions and will usually represent the best value for money when taking care of an asset.

Co-ordinating simple tasks like gutter cleaning and repainting for a terrace as a whole can assist in reducing costs and ensure efficiency, particularly if they are part of an agreed proactive programme of forward management. Further advice for owners is available on the Historic England website.

Works to improve environmental performance, such as additional insulation, need to be carefully considered to avoid unintended consequences for neighbouring properties. Further information on energy efficiency is available on the Historic England website. Works which involve intervention in party walls may require notification under the Party Wall Act.

A wall is a 'party wall' if it stands astride the boundary of land belonging to two (or more) different owners *Party Wall etc Act 1996 Explanatory booklet (MHCLG, May 2016)*

Below are some steps to follow when considering changes to Georgian and Victorian terraced houses:

1. Establish as far as you can the historical and social context of the terrace.

2. Identify the features of the house that are original, with particular reference to plan form. This may include stairs, interior features, roof form, doors and windows and external decoration.

3. Identify opportunities for enhancing the architectural consistency of the terrace as a whole (ie for the different dwellings within the terrace to look similar).

4. Ensure any heritage statement or appraisal provides a clear assessment of what is important and why as well as describing the impact of the proposal. *See* Section 4.1 for more information.

4 Applications for change

4.1 Information for owners

Certain types of change will require planning permission and / or listed building consent. Planning permission is needed for changes which are defined as development. This includes building works, some kinds of demolition and changes of use to existing buildings. For listed buildings, listed building consent will be required for alterations or extensions (including demolition) which affect their character or appearance as a building of special architectural or historic interest.

For more information on permission and consents, please see the Historic England website.

Most routine maintenance and minor repair is unlikely to require listed building consent or planning permission (where relevant) if it is carried out using the same techniques and materials and does not affect the character of the listed building, which could be the individual house or terrace as a whole. It is worth seeking advice on whether or not consent is required (for example, re-painting a stucco terrace might need listed building consent if it was proposed to change the colour).

It is also important to consider whether the significance of the terrace requires an expert assessment to gain the necessary level of understanding. It is good practice for owners/ applicants to seek advice from professionally accredited experts and to comply with relevant standards and guidance.

If the terraced house is unlisted but in a conservation area, there may still be additional controls to protect the historic and architectural elements which make the area special.

For more information on conservation areas, please see the Historic England Advice Note on Conservation Area Appraisal, Designation and Management.

Where a terraced house has been divided into separate dwellings or is defined as a 'House in Multiple Occupation' (HMO) additional requirements may apply and early discussion with the local planning authority is encouraged. Works to floors or ceilings of separate dwellings within the building may be considered party structures under the Party Wall etc Act 1996 and notification may be required.

Figure 11:
Certain types of change to a historic terrace will require permission.

For further information on this complex and changing issue, please see the Planning Portal.

Your home is a House in Multiple Occupation (HMO) if both of the following apply:

■ At least three tenants live there forming more than one household; and

■ You share toilet bathroom or kitchen facilities with other tenants.

4.1.1 Engagement with the local planning authority

When considering proposals for change it is important that owners engage with the local planning authority at an early stage, taking advantage of available pre-application services. To achieve the best outcome from early engagement clear information on what is proposed, supported by simple plans and photographs for example, will help to ensure that the initial discussion is worthwhile for all parties and assist in resolving any issues. It is important for decision makers to take into account the significance of each individual asset when deciding on its capacity for change.

The right information is crucial to good decision making. Applications for change that affect the significance of listed terraces have the best chance of success if they are based upon a good understanding of the particular significance of this type of heritage asset. In making decisions local authorities need to have a clear understanding of the significance of the asset being affected and the potential impact of the proposals. Information on significance is provided by the applicant and can be in the form of a heritage statement on its own or as part of a wider Design and Access Statement if required.

A heritage statement sets out what is important about an asset and why.

The description of the building in the National Heritage List for England provides a starting point and will give the Grade of protection and may include images .Early List Entries were only intended to identify the building but more recent or amended entries provide a fuller account. Some will set out the special architectural and historic interest (key elements of the significance), giving the reasons for the designation, while others are more limited. Adding consideration of context and contemporary circumstances to a heritage statement is advisable in any analysis supporting proposals for change. It is important to note that listing covers a building and its curtilage in its entirety: the interior is covered even if not specifically mentioned. Occasionally, notably since new powers available from 2013, the focus of the special interest may be expressly defined. Any exceptions should be treated with care.

The National Heritage List for England can be used with other sources, including the Local Studies Library, local Record Office, Historic Environment Record, local history societies' records, trade directories and the National Archive which may also provide useful information. The heritage statement does not have to be exhaustive but should be clear on what is important about the asset. The greater the impact the greater the justification for change will need to be. For assets that are particularly complex or significant or applications involving complex proposals further specialist expertise may be required.

4.1.2 Historic England's role

Historic England is a statutory consultee in the planning process. This means that local planning authorities must consult us when considering certain types of planning proposals. These include:

- Listed building consent applications relating to works to a Grade I or II* building, or structural demolition (ie of a staircase, floor structure, roof structure, chimney breast or at least 50% of a principal wall) or demolition of a Grade II building;

- Applications for planning permission for development which affects a Grade I or II* listed building or its setting;

- Development which affects the character or appearance of a Conservation Area and which involves the erection of a new building or the extension of an existing building where the area of land in respect of which the application is made is more than 1,000 square metres.

Your local authority can advise when an application may be notified to Historic England. The local authority makes the final decision about whether to grant permission.

We offer our own pre-application advice service for prospective applicants and details of this can be found on our website.

It is often most effective if a pre-application request to Historic England can be co-ordinated with an approach to the local authority so that a decision on how they will engage with the application, or any fundamental issues, can be resolved at the earliest opportunity. If a local authority indicates that a pre-application discussion with Historic England would assist, requests are made to the relevant Historic England regional office.

5 Further reading

5.1 Historic England publications

Listing Selection Guide Domestic 2: Town Houses

Historic England 2014 *Practical Building Conservation: Building Environment* Surrey and Burlington: Routledge

Historic England 2014 *Practical Building Conservation: Earth, Brick & Terracotta* Surrey and Burlington: Routledge

Historic England 2014 *Practical Building Conservation: Glass & Glazing* Surrey and Burlington: Routledge

Historic England 2014 *Practical Building Conservation: Metals* Surrey and Burlington: Routledge

Historic England 2014 *Practical Building Conservation: Mortars, Renders & Plasters* Surrey and Burlington: Routledge

Good Practice Advice notes (GPAs)

The GPAs provide information on good practice, particularly looking at the principles of how national policy and guidance can be applied.

GPA2: Managing Significance in Decision-Taking in the Historic Environment

GPA3: The Setting of Heritage Assets

Historic England Advice Notes (HEANs)

The HEANs include detailed, practical advice on how to implement national planning policy and guidance.

HEAN 1: Conservation Areas: Designation, Appraisal and Review (Second Edition)

HEAN 2: Making Changes to Heritage Assets

HEAN 5: Setting up a Listed Building Heritage Partnership Agreement

HEAN 7: Local Heritage Listing

HEAN 10: Listed Buildings and Curtilage

5.2 Other publications

Ayres, J 1998 *Building the Georgian City*. New Haven and London: Yale University Press

Burton, N and Guillery, B 2006; *Behind the Façade: London house plans 1660 – 1840*. Reading: Squire Books Ltd

Burton, N, Cruikshank, D et al 1990 *Life in the Georgian City*. London: Viking

Clark, K 2001 *Informed Conservation: understanding historic buildings and their landscapes for conservation*. Swindon: English Heritage

Cruikshank, D and Wyld, P 1975 London: *The art of Georgian building*. London: John Wiley & Sons

Davey, A et al 1995 *The Care and Conservation of Georgian Houses: A maintenance manual for Edinburgh New Town, 4th edition*. Edinburgh: Butterworth Architecture

Guillery, P 2004 *The Small House in Eighteenth Century London*. New Haven and London: Yale University Press

Longstaffe-Gowan, T 2012 *The London Square: gardens in the midst of town*. New Haven and London: Yale University Press

Longstaffe-Gowan, T 2001 *The London Town Garden*. New Haven and London: Yale University Press

Muthesius, S 1984 *The English Terraced House*. New Haven and London: Yale University Press

Stevens Curl, J 2011 *Georgian Architecture in the British Isles 1714 – 1830, 2nd edition*. Swindon: English Heritage

Summerson, J 2003 *Georgian London*, revised edition. New Haven and London: Yale University Press

Calloway, S 2005 *The Elements of Style: an encyclopedia of domestic architectural detail*. London: Mitchell Beazley

5.3 Further sources of advice and information

The Historic England website provides information through webpages and downloadable documents. The Your Home section is specifically aimed at owners of historic buildings. This includes information on:

- Making changes and getting permission

- Saving energy

- Finding a specialist

The National Planning Policy Framework sets out the government's planning policies for England and how these are expected to be applied.

Buildings Conservation Directory

The **Georgian Group** is a conservation organisation created to campaign for the preservation of Georgian buildings and landscapes. Their website contains advice notes on repairing and maintaining various elements of Georgian fabric.

The **Victorian Society** is a charity which champions Victorian and Edwardian buildings in England and Wales. They produce a range of advice documents on caring for Victorian houses which are available to buy and detailed topic reading lists relating to specific aspects of Victorian and Edwardian Architecture.

The **Society for the Protection of Ancient Buildings** (SPAB) website provides information and advice on maintenance, repair and energy efficiency measures.

Contact Historic England

East of England
Brooklands
24 Brooklands Avenue
Cambridge CB2 8BU
Tel: 01223 582749
Email: eastofengland@
HistoricEngland.org.uk

Fort Cumberland
Fort Cumberland Road
Eastney
Portsmouth PO4 9LD
Tel: 023 9285 6704
Email: fort.
cumberland@
HistoricEngland.org.uk

**London and
South East**
4th Floor
Cannon Bridge House
25 Dowgate Hill
London EC4R 2YA
Tel: 020 7973 3700
Email: londonseast@
HistoricEngland.org.uk

Midlands
The Axis
10 Holliday Street
Birmingham B1 1TG
Tel: 0121 625 6888
Email: midlands@
HistoricEngland.org.uk

**North East
and Yorkshire**
Bessie Surtees House
41-44 Sandhill
Newcastle Upon
Tyne NE1 3JF
Tel: 0191 269 1255
Email: northeast@
HistoricEngland.org.uk

37 Tanner Row
York YO1 6WP
Tel: 01904 601948
Email: yorkshire@
HistoricEngland.org.uk

North West
3rd Floor,
Canada House
3 Chepstow Street
Manchester M1 5FW
Tel: 0161 242 1416
Email: northwest@
HistoricEngland.org.uk

South West
29 Queen Square
Bristol BS1 4ND
Tel: 0117 975 1308
Email: southwest@
HistoricEngland.org.uk

Swindon
The Engine House
Fire Fly Avenue
Swindon SN2 2EH
Tel: 01793 445050
Email: swindon@
HistoricEngland.org.uk

Printed and bound by CPI Group (UK) Ltd, Croydon, CR0 4YY